POC
MANUAL

The history of the British monarchy

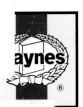

KINGS AND QUEENS

Anita Ganeri has asserted her right to be identified as the
author of this book.

Published in August 2010.

British Library Cataloguing-in-Publication Data:
A catalogue record for this book is available from
the British Library

ISBN 978 1 84425 960 1

Published by Haynes Publishing,
Sparkford, Yeovil, Somerset BA22 7JJ, UK
Tel: 01963 442030 Fax: 01963 440001
Int. tel: +44 1963 442030 Int. fax: +44 1963 440001
Email: sales@haynes.co.uk
Website: www.haynes.co.uk

Haynes North America, Inc.,
861 Lawrence Drive, Newbury Park
California 91320, USA

Design: Richard Parsons

Illustrations: Martin Rowson

Printed and bound in the USA

The Author

Anita Ganeri is an award-winning author of children's information
books, covering a wide range of subjects. In 2009, she won the
Blue Peter Book Award for the Best Book with Facts. She lives in
the north of England with her family and dogs.

POCKET MANUAL

Haynes

The history of the British monarchy

KINGS AND QUEENS

KINGS AND QUEENS
CONTENTS

802-871
EARLY KINGS

EGBERT (802-839)

In the 7th century, Anglo-Saxon England was split into seven kingdoms – Kent, Sussex, Essex, East Anglia, Wessex, Mercia and Northumbria. The kingdoms fought each other for power. Egbert became King of Wessex in 802 and led Wessex to victory against the Mercians and Northumbrians.

ETHELWULF (839-856)

The eldest son of Egbert, Ethelwulf became King of Wessex in 839. During his reign, he and his sons fought many battles against Viking raiders from Denmark. Deeply religious, he also made a pilgrimage to Rome.

ETHELBALD (856-860)
ETHELBERT (860-866)
ETHELRED I (865-871)

Four of Ethelwulf's five sons became king after him. Ethelbald and Ethelbert ruled Wessex and Kent while their father was in Rome, and later succeeded him. Etheldred continued to fight the Vikings but was killed in battle in April 871.

TURNING POINT

ANGLO-SAXONS

In the 5th century, the Romans left Britain after 400 years of rule. New settlers from Europe began to invade. They became known as the Anglo-Saxons.

TIMELINE

	802 Egbert becomes King of Wessex
c769 Birth of Egbert	
c795 Birth of Ethelwulf	**c834** Birth of Ethelbald
	c835 Birth of Ethelbert

c837 Birth of Ethelred
839 Death of Egbert; Ethelwulf becomes King of Wessex

DID YOU KNOW?
In 843 Kenneth MacAlpin, King of the Scots, united the kingdoms of the Picts and the Scots. They became known as Scotland.

EGBERT

| 856 | Death of Ethelwulf; Ethelbald becomes king | 860 | Death of Ethelbald; Ethelbert becomes king | 865 | Death of Ethelbert; Ethelred becomes king |
| | | | | 871 | Death of Ethelred; Alfred becomes king |

871-899
ALFRED THE GREAT

The only English king known as 'Great', Alfred was the youngest son of Ethelwulf (see page 6). He came to the throne of Wessex in 871, when his brother, Ethelred (see page 6), died. A wise and learned ruler, he fought against the Danish invasion and was a great champion of art and literature and legal reformer.

STRUGGLE AGAINST THE VIKINGS

From the end of the 8th century, Vikings from Denmark raided England. In 878, led by King Guthrum, they invaded Wessex. Alfred was forced into hiding but later defeated Guthrum. In 886, Alfred captured London. He was declared king of all of England that was not under Danish rule.

TURNING POINT

ANGLO-SAXON CHRONICLE

The Anglo-Saxon Chronicle is a collection of writings begun during Alfred's reign. It is one of the most important sources of Anglo-Saxon history. Copies were kept in monasteries across England, and several still survive.

TIMELINE

c849	Birth of Alfred in Oxfordshire, England
871	Becomes King of Wessex, on death of brother, Ethelred I.
878	Defeats the Danes
886	Captures London
899	Dies, probably in Wessex

DID YOU KNOW?

A story tells how, while hiding in a cowherd's cottage, Alfred was left to watch over some cakes (bread). Deep in thought, he did not notice them burning. The man's wife was furious with Alfred, not realising who he was.

899-924
EDWARD THE ELDER

Alfred the Great died in 899 and was succeeded by his son, Edward. A great soldier, Edward continued his father's work, fighting the Vikings and extending Wessex's power. By 920, he had conquered Mercia and East Anglia and pushed as far north as the River Humber.

924-939
ATHELSTAN

The son of Edward the Elder, Athelstan was brought up in Mercia by his aunt, Aethelfleda. On Edward's death, Athelstan became King of Mercia, then of Wessex. A great soldier, he seized York, then Northumbria and extended the boundaries of his kingdom. He also drew up new codes of laws, and set up national assemblies across the country.

TURNING POINT

BATTLE OF BRUNANBURH

In 937, an army of Irish Vikings and Scots invaded England. At the Battle of Brunanburh, they were defeated by Athelstan. This settled his position as King of England.

TIMELINE

	899 Edward becomes King of Wessex	925 Athelstan crowned King of Wessex	
c875 Birth of Edward in Wessex	924 Edward dies in Cheshire		
c895 Birth of Athelstan in Wessex	924 Athelstan crowned King of Mercia	937 Battle of Brunanburh	
		939 Death of Athelstan	

DID YOU KNOW?

Athelstan was a devout Christian and a great collector of religious relics. Among them, he is said to have had a fragment of the cross on which Jesus Christ was crucified.

ATHELSTAN

939-946
EDMUND I

Edmund I was Athelstan's half brother and son of Edward the Elder. Having fought at Brunanburh, he faced another military threat on becoming king, when the Vikings regained control of York and Northumbria. Later, on the death of Olaf, the Viking king, Edmund was able to retake much of the territory he had lost.

946-955
EDRED

Edred was the third of Edward the Elder's sons to rule. During his reign, York fell to the Vikings again, under their king, Erik Bloodaxe. Erik was driven out, and later murdered by Edred's men. A sick man, Edred died in 955, at the age of 32. He was succeeded by his nephew, Eadwig, son of Edmund I.

TIMELINE

939 Edmund becomes king		
921 Birth of Edmund in Wessex	**941** Birth of Edwy	**946** Death of Edmund; Edred becomes king
923 Birth of Edred	**c942** Birth of Edgar	

955-959
EDWY

Edwy became king when he was just 15. He died four years later but his short reign was marked by conflicts with his family, the nobles and the Church. In 957, the kingdom was split between Edwy and his younger brother, Edgar, who was declared King of Mercia and Northumbria.

959-975
EDGAR

Edgar succeeded his brother, Eadwig, and reunited England. His reign was largely peaceful. He brought Dunstan back from exile and made him Archbishop of Canterbury and his chief adviser. The monasteries flourished and became centres of learning and culture.

955 Death of Edred; Edwy becomes king	**957** Edgar becomes King of Mercia and Northumbria	**959** Edgar becomes King of Wessex
	959 Death of Edwy	**975** Death of Edgar

975-978
EDWARD THE MARTYR

Edgar's son, Edward was a teenager when his father died suddenly and he became king. Just three years later, Edward was murdered by a servant while visiting his brother and archrival, Ethelred, and stepmother at Corfe Castle. His tomb was later associated with miracles and he was declared a saint.

> ...While he was eagerly drinking from the cup which had been presented, the dagger of an attendant pierce him through.
>
> WILLIAM OF MALMESBURY

TIMELINE

c962 Birth of Edward the Martyr

c968 Birth of Ethelred

975 Death of Edgar

975 Edward becomes king

978-1016
ETHELRED II

A weak and ill-advised king, Ethelred was unlucky that his reign saw the return of the Viking threat. After a heavy defeat, Ethelred agreed to pay tribute (called the Danegeld) in return for peace. In 1014, an invasion, led by Sweyn Forkbeard, King of Denmark, forced Ethelred to flee to France, though he later returned as king.

DID YOU KNOW?

In Old English, Ethelred's name means 'good counsel' but he was nicknamed 'unready', a twist on his name that means the opposite.

| 978 | Murder of Edward; Ethelred becomes king | 1001 | Edward declared a saint | 1016 | Death of Ethelred |

1016-1035
CANUTE

With Ethelred in exile, Sweyn Forkbeard was declared King of England. His reign lasted for just six weeks and he died in 1014. Two years later, his son, Canute, returned from Denmark to England to fight for the throne. When Ethelred died, the kingdom was split between his son, Edmund, and Canute. Edmund died, a few months later, leaving Canute as King of England.

CANUTE'S REIGN

Canute was King of England, Denmark and Norway, and one of the most powerful men in Europe. A strong ruler, he treated his subjects fairly and brought much-needed stability to England, after a period of bloody fighting. He appointed earls to help govern the kingdom, and modernised the laws. Art, trade and the Church flourished.

TURNING POINT

TURNING BACK THE TIDE

A famous story about Canute tells how he tried, and failed, to turn back the tide. His followers had been boasting about how powerful the king was and he wanted to show them that his power was not as great as they believed.

TIMELINE

c995   Birth of Canute

1013   Reign of Sweyn Forkbeard

1014   Ethelred restored to throne

1016   Death of Ethelred

1016   Edmund Ironside and Canute rule; Edmund dies

1035   Death of Canute

...I have never spared — nor will I spare in the future — to devote myself and my toil for the need and benefit of all my people.

CANUTE LETTER

1035-1040
HAROLD I 'HAREFOOT'

Following Canute's death, his two sons, Harold and Hardicanute, fought to succeed him. While Hardicanute was away in Denmark, Harold seized the throne and became King of England. In 1036, Alfred, son of Ethelred II (see page 15), launched an invasion but was captured and brutally murdered. Harold died in 1040.

DID YOU KNOW?

When Harold died, Hardicanute dug up his brother's body, beheaded his corpse and tossed his head into a marsh near the River Thames. It was later found by a fisherman and buried in a Danish cemetery in London.

TIMELINE

C1012	Birth of Harold	1028	Hardicanute becomes King of Denmark	1035	Harold becomes King of England
1018	Birth of Hardicanute				

1040–1042
HARDICANUTE

From Denmark, Hardicanute assembled a fleet to conquer England and take the throne from Harold. But, in the meantime, Harold died and Hardicanute became the undisputed King of England. He immediately raised taxes to pay for his army and navy, leading to great unrest. Hardicanute died in 1042, after drinking to excess at a wedding.

TURNING POINT

A SUCCESSOR

The year before Hardicanute died, he invited his half-brother, Edward, to court and seems to have appointed him his successor. Edward was the son of Aethelred II and Emma of Normandy, Hardicanute's mother who later married Canute.

1040 Harold dies; Hardicanute becomes king

1042 Death of Hardicanute

1042-1066
EDWARD THE CONFESSOR

The oldest surviving son of Ethelred II, Edward was exiled to Normandy, France, as a child. In 1041, he was asked to return by Hardicanute, and proclaimed king when Hardicanute died a year later.

POWER STRUGGLE

The early part of Edward's reign was marked by a power struggle with Godwine of Essex, the most powerful English earl. To strengthen his position, Godwine gave his daughter to Edward in marriage. In 1051, Edward sent Godwine into exile but he returned the following year to threaten the king. Godwine died in 1053, leaving Edward once more in charge.

TURNING POINT

TWO HEIRS

Edward did not have any children. When he died, two men fought for his throne – Duke William of Normandy (Edward's cousin) and Harold Godwineson (son of Godwine). Their struggle for power led to the Norman Conquest of England (see page 22)

TIMELINE

c1005 Birth of Edward

1042 Edward becomes king

1043 Coronation in Winchester Cathedral

c1050 Rebuilding of Westminster Abbey begins

1066 Death of Edward

DID YOU KNOW?

Deeply religious, Edward was made a saint in 1161. Two years later, his body was buried in a shrine in Westminster Abbey.

1066
HAROLD II

Harold became Earl of Wessex in 1063, on his father's death. When Edward (see page 20) died in January 1066, Harold was declared king. In September, he faced an invasion by the Norwegian king, Harald Hardrada, but defeated Harald at the Battle of Stamford Bridge in Yorkshire. Almost immediately, Harold led his army south to face an even greater threat.

THE BATTLE OF HASTINGS

On 28 September, William, Duke of Normandy, landed on the south coast of England with several thousand men. Two weeks later, his army faced Harold at the Battle of Hastings. The battle lasted all day, with heavy losses on each side. Eventually, Harold was killed, possibly by an arrow through his eye.

TURNING POINT

NORMAN CONQUEST
The Normans were originally Vikings from Scandinavia who settled in Normandy in the 10th century and adopted the French language and customs.

TIMELINE

c1022	Birth of Harold II
1063	Becomes Earl of Wessex

1066 (January) Death of Edward the Confessor; Harold becomes king; (September)

Battle of Stamford Bridge; (October) Death of Harold at Battle of Hastings William becomes king

DID YOU KNOW?

Halley's Comet appeared in the sky on the day of Harold's coronation in Westminster Abbey. This was seen as an omen of disaster.

1066-1087
WILLIAM I

William's victory marked the end of Anglo-Saxon England. He was crowned king on Christmas Day 1066, and set about bringing England under Norman control. Norman nobles seized Anglo-Saxon lands, and took over positions of power. French became the language of government. Rebellions were ruthlessly crushed, and tens of thousands of people killed.

WILLIAM THE CONQUEROR DIES

William became known as 'the Conqueror' but the last years of his reign were quite peaceful. He himself spent most of his time in France where he died in 1087 after falling from his horse. He was buried in the city of Caen

TURNING POINT

DOMESDAY BOOK

In 1085, William ordered a survey of his new kingdom. He wanted to know how much it was worth and how much tax he could raise. The result became known as the Domesday Book. It gives a remarkably detailed record of landowners, their land and livestock.

TIMELINE

c1027 Birth of William I
1066 Death of Edward the Confessor

1066 Harold becomes king; Death of Harold at Battle of Hastings;

1066 William becomes king
1087 Death of William I

DID YOU KNOW?

The Bayeux Tapestry is a long embroidered cloth which tells the story of the Norman Conquest of England. Legend says that it was stitched by William's wife, Matilda.

1087-1100
WILLIAM II

When William the Conqueror died in 1087, his lands were divided between two of his sons. Robert became Duke of Normandy, and William became King of England. Known as William Rufus, because of his red-faced appearance and fiery temper, William II was a ruthless and unpopular king. He taxed his subjects heavily, and quarrelled with the Church.

RUTHLESS RULER

Early in his reign, William crushed a rebellion of Norman nobles who supported his brother. He later did a deal with Robert and took charge of Normandy. William also faced invasions from Scotland, led by the Scottish king, Malcolm III. In 1093, he crushed the Scots at Alnwick, and killed Malcolm. In 1097, he put down another revolt, in Wales.

TURNING POINT

WILLIAM'S DEATH

William died on 2 August 1100, while out hunting. He was shot by an arrow, supposedly by accident. But he may have been assassinated on the orders of his younger brother, Henry (later Henry I).

TIMELINE

1087 Becomes King of England	**1093** Defeats the Scots
c1056 Birth of William II	**1088** Crushes a revolt in Normandy	**1100** Death of William II

DID YOU KNOW?

Even as children, William and Robert did not get on. A story tells how William and his younger brother, Henry, emptied a stinking chamber pot over Robert's head.

1100–1135
HENRY I

The third son of William the Conqueror, Henry was left a large sum of money when his father died, but no lands. When his brother, William Rufus, was killed, Henry seized his chance. While his other brother, Robert, was away at the Crusades, Henry rushed to London and had himself crowned king.

STABLE GOVERNMENT

Henry I was an intelligent and good ruler, and immediately set about winning back people's support. A Charter of Liberties was drawn up, to put right the injustices of his brother's reign. He also reformed the royal treasury and made peace with the Church. Henry was less generous towards his brother, Robert. He defeated him at the Battle of Tinchebrai in 1106, and kept him prisoner until his death.

TURNING POINT

FATAL SHIPWRECK

Disaster struck in 1120. Henry's son and heir, William, was drowned when his ship hit a rock and sunk. It is said that the king was so grief-stricken, he never smiled again. He named his daughter, Matilda, as his successor.

TIMELINE

1068 Birth of Henry I	**1106** Defeats Robert at Battle of Tinchebrai	**1120** Son, William, drowns at sea
1100 Becomes King of England		**1135** Death of Henry I

DID YOU KNOW?

Henry died in France from food poisoning, after eating a plate of lampreys (eel-like fish), against his doctor's orders.

1135–1154
STEPHEN

When Henry I died, his daughter and heir, Matilda, was in France. Before she could return to England, her cousin, Stephen, claimed the throne. Crucially, he was backed by the barons who did not like the idea of being ruled by a woman. Nineteen years of chaos and bloody civil war followed, known as 'the Anarchy', as Stephen and Matilda fought for the crown.

QUEEN MATILDA

In 1139, Matilda invaded England. Two years' later, her forces captured Stephen at the Battle of Lincoln. Matilda finally became queen for a few months, although she was never crowned. Stephen was later freed, in exchange for one of Matilda's most trusted advisors, and restored to the throne. Matilda returned to France in 1148.

TURNING POINT

TREATY OF WALLINGFORD

The civil war ended in 1153, with the Treaty of Wallingford. Under the terms of the Treaty, it was agreed that Stephen would stay king as long as he lived. Then the throne would pass to Matilda's son, Henry of Anjou.

TIMELINE

1102	Birth of Matilda
1135	Stephen becomes king
c1096	Birth of Stephen
1153	Treaty of Wallingford
1154	Death of Stephen
1167	Death of Matilda

DID YOU KNOW?

Stephen almost captured Matilda near Oxford. Under cover of darkness, she made a dramatic escape, dressed in a white cloak to camouflage her against the snow.

1154–1189
HENRY II

On his father's death, and through marriage to Eleanor of Aquitaine, Henry became ruler of large parts of France. Then, in 1154, he added England to his vast empire. Tough, strong, hot-tempered and intelligent, Henry II proved a great ruler. After Stephen's rule, he set out restoring order and reforming the country's legal and religious systems.

CHURCH REFORM

In 1164, Henry set out his religious reforms which were fiercely opposed by the Church. Henry quarrelled with Thomas à Becket, the Archbishop of Canterbury, over the new laws. Exasperated, Henry shouted, 'Will no one rid me of this turbulent priest?' He was overheard by four knights who set off for Canterbury to murder Becket. Filled with remorse, Henry did penance by walking barefoot to Canterbury, wearing a hair shirt. Becket was later made a saint.

TURNING POINT

TRIAL BY JURY

As part of his legal reforms, Henry II brought in trial by jury for the first time – the system we still use today. It replaced trial by ordeal and trial by combat, and was much fairer, faster and more reliable.

TIMELINE

1133	Birth of Henry II
1152	Marries Eleanor of Aquitaine
1154	Becomes King of England
1170	Murder of Thomas à Becket
1171	Becomes Lord of Ireland
1189	Death of Henry II

DID YOU KNOW?

Henry II was the first king of the Plantagenet dynasty that ruled England for more than 300 years. 'Plantagenet' was his father, Geoffrey's, nickname. He liked to wear a spring of broom, or planta genista, in his helmet.

1189-1199
RICHARD I

Henry II's last years were plagued by family quarrels. In 1183, he was forced to name his son, Richard, Duke of Aquitaine, as his heir. Henry wanted Richard to hand Aquitaine over to his youngest son, John. Richard refused and joined forces with Philip II of France against his father. When Henry died in 1189, Richard became King of England.

LIONHEART

Soon afterwards, Richard, a fine soldier, set off to the Holy Land to join the Third Crusade. His exploits later earned him the nickname 'Coeur de Lion' or 'Lionheart'. Despite several victories, he was not able to win back Jerusalem. Running short of men and money, he made peace with Saladin, the Muslim leader. On his way home, Richard was captured by the German emperor, Henry VI who demanded a huge ransom for Richard's freedom. This was raised, at great cost, in England.

TURNING POINT

THE CRUSADES

The Crusades were wars fought between Christians and Muslims for control of Jerusalem and other holy sites in Palestine. They began in 1095, when the Pope appealed for fighters to go to the Holy Land. Known as Crusades, from the Latin word 'crux' for cross.

TIMELINE

1157	Birth of Richard I	
1189	Becomes King of England	
1189	Joins the Third Crusade	
1191	Reaches the Holy Land	
1192	Taken prisoner in Germany	
1194	Released and returns home	
1199	Death of Richard I	

DID YOU KNOW?

Legend says that Richard's servant found out where the king was being kept prisoner by singing his favourite song outside castles in Germany. Eventually he heard Richard's voice joining in.

1199-1216
JOHN

The youngest son of Henry II, John became king on the death of his brother, Richard I. Already unpopular, John's reign began disastrously. He lost his lands in France, earning the nickname of 'Softsword' for his failure as a soldier. He then began taxing his subjects heavily, to pay for a great war to win his French lands back.

THE BARONS REBEL

In 1215, the English people, led by the barons rebelled against the high taxes. The barons demanded King John meet them at Runnymede by the River Thames. There, they forced him to put his seal to the Magna Carta. But no sooner had John agreed than he went back on his word.

> "No man can ever trust him For his heart is soft and cowardly!
FROM A SONG ABOUT KING JOHN

TURNING POINT

MAGNA CARTA

The Magna Carta was the first treaty to set down rules for how a monarch should rule. In it, John agreed to treat people more fairly and to appoint a committee to whom people could complain if they felt the king was not keeping his promises.

TIMELINE

1166 Birth of John	**1199** Becomes King of England	**1215** Sealing of the Magna Carta
		1216 Death of John

DID YOU KNOW?

King John is famous for losing the Crown Jewels as he was crossing the Wash, a marshy estuary on the east coast of England. The tide came in and swept them out to sea.

1216-1272
HENRY III

Henry was only nine years old when his father, John, died and he became king. Regents ruled in his name until he was old enough to take power. His reign lasted for 56 years. Despite this, he was not a particularly popular king but was seen as weak, indecisive and inefficient.

THE BARONS REBEL

Henry III soon found himself in conflict with the barons. They resented the favours he showed to his French relations and his lack of regard for the Magna Carta. Led by Simon de Montfort they forced him to agree to a set of documents, called the Provisions of Oxford. These created a council of 15 barons to advise the king and oversee the government. In 1264, civil war broke out. De Montfort captured the king and a year later, called a parliament. For the first time, it included not only nobles but also knights, merchants and clergymen.

BATTLE OF EVESHAM

In May 1265, Prince Edward (later King Edward I) escaped from prison and led his army against De Montfort. In August, he defeated and killed De Montfort at the Battle of Evesham, restoring royal authority.

TIMELINE

1207 Birth of Henry III	**1258** Provisions of Oxford	**1265** Battle of Evesham
1216 Becomes King of England	**1265** First English Parliament;	**1272** Death of Henry III

DID YOU KNOW?

Henry greatly admired St Edward the Confessor and had a mural of him painted in his bedchamber.

1272-1307
EDWARD I

Prince Edward was on his way home from the Crusades when he learned that his father, Henry III, had died. He reached London in 1274, and was crowned king. Unlike his father, Edward I was brave, athletic and a great soldier. He was also tall, with long arms and legs, which earned him the nickname 'Edward Longshanks'.

UNITED KINGDOMS

Much of Edward's reign was spent fighting. He crushed one Welsh revolt in 1277, and another in 1282. Two years later, Wales became part of England. In Scotland, Edward backed John Balliol to be king, angering the Scottish nobles. They rebelled and, in 1296, Edward marched north to invade. A year later, William Wallace led the Scots against the English but was eventually defeated. In 1306, Robert the Bruce was crowned King of Scotland. Edward was on his way north to fight Bruce when he died in 1307.

TURNING POINT

WILLIAM WALLACE

William Wallace was a knight who became a Scottish hero. Leading the Scottish forces, Wallace won a famous victory over the English at the Battle of Stirling Bridge in 1297. In 1305, Wallace was captured and taken to London, where he was tried for treason and executed.

TIMELINE

1239	Birth of Edward I	**1274**	Crowned in Westminster Abbey
1272	Becomes King of England	**1284**	Wales becomes part of England
		1297	Battle of Stirling Bridge
		1298	Battle of Falkirk
		1307	Death of Edward II

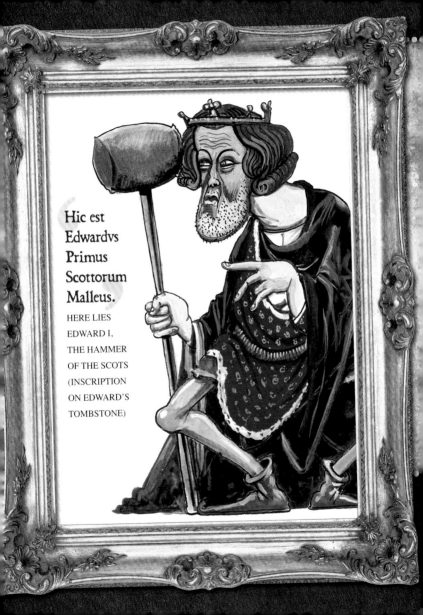

Hic est
Edwardvs
Primus
Scottorum
Malleus.

HERE LIES
EDWARD I,
THE HAMMER
OF THE SCOTS
(INSCRIPTION
ON EDWARD'S
TOMBSTONE)

1307-1327
EDWARD II

Edward was born in 1284. The fourth, and only surviving, son of Edward I, he became king in 1307. From the beginning, his 20-year reign ran into trouble. His closest friend, Piers Gaveston, was deeply unpopular, and finally put to death. In 1311, a set of reforms, called the Ordinances, was issued to limit the king's power and spending.

EDWARD II IS OVERTHROWN

In 1326, Edward's wife, Isabella, returned to France. Together with her lover, Roger Mortimer, she raised an army to invade England. Edward was captured, deposed, in favour of his son, and imprisoned in Berkeley Castle. It is said he was kept in a cell over a pit of animal corpses, in the hope that the smell or disease would kill him. It did not, and he was later murdered.

TURNING POINT

BATTLE OF BANNOCKBURN

In Scotland, Robert the Bruce steadily won back the lands lost to Edward I. Finally, in 1314, Edward II led his English army north. The two sides met at Bannockburn, outside Stirling, on 23 June. Despite being heavily outnumbered, the Scots were victorious. Edward was forced to flee back to England.

TIMELINE

1284	Birth of Edward II
1307	Becomes King of England
1308	Marries Isabella of France
1314	Battle of Bannockburn
1322	Battle of Boroughbridge
1327	Edward II is deposed

DID YOU KNOW?

In 1302, Edward was made Prince of Wales by his father, Edward I. Ever since that time, the British monarch's eldest son has been given this title.

1327–1377
EDWARD III

Edward III was a 14-year-old boy when his father, Edward II, was deposed. His reign lasted for 50 years. At first, his mother and Roger Mortimer (see page 42) ruled in his name. Then Edward took power, had Mortimer executed and his mother imprisoned for life. Tall, handsome and generous, Edward was hugely popular with his subjects.

100 YEARS' WAR

Edward's reign was dominated by the 100 Years War with France (It actually lasted for 116 years). Edward claimed the French throne because his mother, Isabella, was daughter of King Philip IV of France. His armies famously defeated the French at Crecy and Poitiers, and gained control of Calais. But the war was costly, and, as the Black Death raged across England, there was a shortage of soldiers. In 1360, Edward accepted the Treaty of Bretigny, giving up his claim in return for substantial lands.

TURNING POINT

ORDER OF THE GARTER

In 1348, Edward III created the Order of the Garter, a society of knights that still exists today. It has only 24 members, including the monarch and the Prince of Wales. A story tells how a lady dancing accidentally dropped her garter. The king picked it up and tied it around his own leg.

TIMELINE

	1327 Becomes King of England	**1346** Battle of Crecy
		1356 Battle of Poitiers
1312 Birth of Edward III	**1337** Start of 100 Years' War	**1376** Death of the Black Prince
		1377 Death of Edward III

DID YOU KNOW?

At the Battle of Poitiers, the English were commanded by Edward III's son, Edward, Prince of Wales. Known as the 'Black Prince' because of the colour of his armour.

1377-1399
RICHARD II

The son of the Black Prince, Richard was 10 years old when his grandfather, Edward III, died and he became king. The country was ruled largely by Richard's uncle, John of Gaunt. Richard faced his first crisis in 1381 with the Peasants' Revolt. Despite being only 14 years old, he faced the rebels bravely.

A KING'S DOWNFALL

Richard soon ran into trouble and a group of nobles tried to limit his royal powers. They also disliked Richard's friends, and had some of them executed. Richard waited, then took his revenge. He had his chief enemies put to death, and his cousin, Henry Bolingroke, son of John of Gaunt, banished. When Gaunt died in 1399, he confiscated his vast estates in Lancashire. With Richard away fighting in Ireland, Bolingbroke invaded England. Richard was forced to abdicate, leaving Bolingbroke to be crowned King.

TURNING POINT

PEASANTS' REVOLT

In 1381, around 100,000 men marched from Kent to London to protest against the hated poll tax, raised to pay for the wars in France. Richard met the rebel leader, Wat Tyler, and agreed to grant his requests. But Richard later went back on his promises, and the rebels were hunted down and killed.

TIMELINE

		1377	Becomes King of England	1400	Richard II dies in Pontefract Castle
1367	Birth of Richard II	1381	Peasants' Revolt		
		1399	Richard abdicates		

DID YOU KNOW?

Richard liked to dress in sumptuous clothes and extravagant jewels. He is said to have introduced the use of pocket handkerchiefs at court.

1399-1413
HENRY IV

The first of three kings of the House of Lancaster, Henry IV was the eldest son of John of Gaunt. A fine soldier and able ruler, he also made many enemies, and his reign was marked by almost constant warfare.

REVOLTS AND REBELLIONS

In 1401, Owen Glendower led a Welsh rebellion against English rule. He was joined by Henry Percy, Earl of Northumberland. Once Henry IV's loyal supporter, he and his son, Harry Hotspur, now turned against the king. But Glendower and Percy were defeated, and Hotspur killed, at the Battle of Shrewsbury. Several further rebellions followed, but faded when Percy was killed in 1408.

TURNING POINT

OWEN GLENDOWER

The legendary leader of the Welsh rebellion, Owen Glendower (Owain Glyndwr), was born in around 1354. A wealthy landowner, he claimed to be descended from the ancient princes of Wales. Glendower was last seen alive in 1412. Despite the offer of huge rewards, he was never captured, and his final years remain a mystery.

TIMELINE

		1399	Becomes King of England	1403	Battle of Shrewsbury
		1401	Start of Welsh revolt	1413	Death of Henry IV
1366	Birth of Henry IV				

DID YOU KNOW?

A series of bad omens marked Henry IV's coronation ceremony. For example, one of the king's golden spurs fell off, said to be a sign that rebellion was on the way.

1413-1422
HENRY V

The son of Henry IV, Henry came to the throne in 1413. As Prince of Wales, he had already proved himself to be a great soldier, fighting against the Welsh rebels. He was also a shrewd politician. As his father's health grew worse, Henry played an ever larger part in governing the country.

FIGHTING IN FRANCE

Within a few years of becoming king, Henry V sailed to France to win back the lands lost by his ancestors. The campaign was a great success. In September 1415, he captured Harfleur, the leading port in north-west France. This was followed by a dazzling victory at the Battle of Agincourt. Further English successes followed, and, in 1419, Henry captured Rouen. By 1420, the French were forced to agree to the Treaty of Troyes (see box).

TURNING POINT

TREATY OF TROYES

Under the terms of the Treaty of Troyes, Henry became regent of France and heir to the French throne. Charles VI, the French king, also gave Henry the hand of his daughter, Catherine, in marriage. Henry died, before he could be crowned.

TIMELINE

1387	Birth of Henry V
1413	Becomes King of England
1415	Battle of Agincourt (25 October)
1419	Siege of Rouen
1420	Treaty of Troyes
1422	Death of Henry V

DID YOU KNOW?

A story says that a furious Henry invaded France after being sent a gift of tennis balls by the French. Their message was that Henry should stick to playing games until he was old enough to take part in war.

1422-1461
HENRY VI

By the age of 12 months, Henry VI was King of England and France. Regents governed both countries until Henry was old enough to rule for himself. A gentle and deeply religious man, Henry was a poor politician who hated war. Surrounded by powerful nobles, he could not prevent power struggles breaking out at court.

LOSSES IN FRANCE

Henry was crowned King of England in 1429, and of France in 1432. The 100 Years' War was still raging and the French, inspired by Joan of Arc (see box), were gaining ground. By 1450, England had lost Normandy and Aquitaine. By 1453, only Calais remained in English hands. Resentment against the king and his weak government grew.

TURNING POINT

MARGARET OF ANJOU

Henry married Margaret of Anjou in 1445. She proved to be a strong and determined queen, leading the Lancastrian forces against the Yorkists during Henry's illness. Defeated at the Battle of Tewkesbury, she was held prisoner until the French king paid a ransom. She died in France in 1482.

TIMELINE

1421 Birth of Henry VI

1422 Becomes King of England and France

1437 Henry VI takes power

1440 Founds Eton College

DID YOU KNOW?

Well-educated himself, Henry VI was a great supporter of learning and culture. He founded the famous public school, Eton College, in 1440, and King's College, Cambridge (University) in 1447.

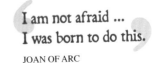

'I am not afraid ...
I was born to do this.

JOAN OF ARC

JOAN OF ARC

DID YOU KNOW?

The Wars of the Roses were later given their name because the Lancastrians' emblem was a red rose, and the Yorkists' a white rose.

TURNING POINT

JOAN OF ARC

Joan of Arc was a young French peasant girl. In 1429, she claimed to have had a vision of the Virgin Mary telling her to drive the English out of France. She was later captured by the English, and, in 1431, was accused of being a witch and burned at the stake.

WARS OF THE ROSES

In 1453, Henry's health broke down, and Richard, Duke of York, took charge. By 1455, Henry had partly recovered but war broke out between his Lancastrian forces and the Yorkists, led by Richard. The following struggle is known as the Wars of the Roses (see box). In 1460, Richard was killed at the Battle of Wakefield but, a year later, his son, Edward, defeated the Lancastrians and was crowned king. Henry was captured but, with the help of the Earl of Warwick, was restored to the throne in 1470. His second reign lasted for only a few months. At the Battle of Tewkesbury in May 1471, the Lancastrians were ruthlessly crushed. Henry was murdered a few months later, in the Tower of London.

| 1445 | Marries Margaret of Anjou | 1455 | Wars of the Roses begin | 1470 | Restored to throne |
| 1447 | Founds King's College, Cambridge | 1461 | Deposed; Edward IV crowned | 1471 | Deposed (April); murdered (May) |

1461-1470; 1471-1483
EDWARD IV

The first Yorkist king, Edward IV was intelligent, ruthless, and had already proved himself a great soldier during the Wars of the Roses. His reign was split into two parts. The first was dominated by the war. The second saw England peaceful and prosperous again. Edward revived overseas trade and improved the royal finances.

THE EARL OF WESSEX

Richard Neville, Earl of Warwick, was the richest and most powerful nobleman in England. Originally a supporter of Richard of York, he was a key figure in making Edward king. But, finding he could not control Edward, he turned against him and helped to restore Henry VI to the throne (see pages 55). This earned him the nickname of 'Warwick the Kingmaker'.

DID YOU KNOW?

In 1477, Edward fell out with his brother, George, and accused him of treason. The following year, he had George killed – supposedly by drowning him in a barrel of wine..

TIMELINE

1442	Birth of Edward IV
1461	Becomes King of England
1470	Edward IV deposed
1471	Edward IV restored to throne
1483	Death of Edward IV (April); Edward V becomes king

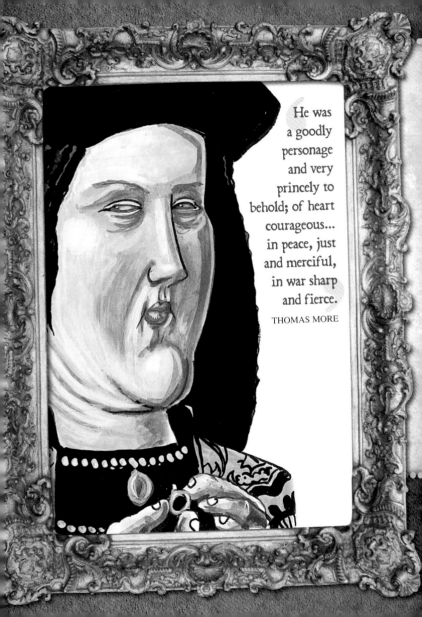

He was
a goodly
personage
and very
princely to
behold; of heart
courageous...
in peace, just
and merciful,
in war sharp
and fierce.

THOMAS MORE

1483
EDWARD V

When Edward IV died in 1483, his crown passed to his son, Edward. But, before Edward could be crowned, he and his younger brother, Richard, were declared illegitimate and deposed. Their uncle, Richard, Duke of Gloucester, became Richard III. Soon afterwards, Edward and Richard disappeared from the Tower of London and were never seen again.

DID YOU KNOW?

In 1674, two skeletons were found in the Tower and were buried in Westminster Abbey. They were examined again in 1933 but experts could not say for certain if they belonged to the two young princes.

TURNING POINT

PRINCE OF WALES

Edward became Prince of Wales in 1471, when he was just a year old. He was brought up in Ludlow, Shropshire, by his uncle, Lord Rivers. When his father died, he and Rivers set off for London. On the way, they were met by Richard who took Edward into his care and lodged him, and his younger brother, in the Tower.

TIMELINE

1470 Birth of Edward V

1471 Edward becomes Prince of Wales

1483 (April) Becomes king; (June) Deposed; (August) Death of Edward

1483-1485
RICHARD III

The son of Richard of York, Richard fought beside his brother, Edward, and helped him to defeat Henry VI. When Edward became king, Richard was made Duke of Gloucester and rewarded with lands in northern England. Richard became king in 1483, and moved quickly to crush a rebellion by his former supporter, the Duke of Buckingham.

BATTLE OF BOSWORTH FIELD

Richard soon faced a more serious revolt by the Lancastrian Earl of Richmond, Henry Tudor. Henry landed in Wales, marched east and met Richard on 22 August 1485, at the Battle of Bosworth Field in Leicestershire. Finding himself cut off and outnumbered, Richard refused to flee and was killed. Henry Tudor seized the throne as Henry VII (see page 62), bringing the War of the Roses to an end.

TURNING POINT

RICHARD'S REPUTATION

Later accounts of Richard painted a picture of an evil villain, who had the princes in the Tower murdered. He was also said to have had a crooked back and a limp. But these were most likely the work of writers who supported the Tudors. Modern historians question whether Richard really deserved his bad reputation.

TIMELINE

		1461	Made Duke of Gloucester	1483	Becomes King of England
1452	Birth of Richard III	1472	Marries Anne Neville	1485	Dies at Battle of Bosworth Field

DID YOU KNOW?
After Richard's death at the
Battle of Bosworth Field, it
is said that the crown of
England was found
lying under a
hawthorn
tree.

1485-1509
HENRY VII

The son of Edmund Tudor, the Lancastrian Earl of Richmond, Henry fled into exile in France in 1471, when the Yorkist Edward IV retook the throne. On his return in 1485, he defeated Richard III at Bosworth Field and became king. Henry took a firm grip on government, and, when he died in 1509, he left a reasonably secure and prosperous kingdom.

FAMILY LIFE

In 1486, Henry married Elizabeth of York, daughter of Edward IV, uniting the two sides of the Wars of the Roses. Henry also joined the rose symbols of York and Lancaster into a new Tudor emblem. Henry and Elizabeth had six children but only three outlived their father. Henry's eldest son, Prince Arthur, died in 1503, leaving his younger brother, Henry (the future Henry VIII) to become heir to the throne.

TURNING POINT

THE TUDORS

Henry VII was the first king of the Tudor dynasty that marked the end of the Middle Ages in England. He was the first of five Tudor monarchs that included some of the most famous kings and queens in English history.

TIMELINE

1457	Birth of Henry Tudor	**1472**	Exiled to France	**1485**	Becomes King of England
		1485	Battle of Bosworth Field		

DID YOU KNOW?

When Henry VII died, he left enough money so that 10,000 masses could be said for the good of his soul.

ELIZABETH OF YORK

DID YOU KNOW?

The word 'football' was coined in Henry VII's reign. It may have described a ball-kicking game played on foot by peasants, rather than on horseback, by nobles.

TURNING POINT

IMPOSTERS

In 1487, Henry crushed a revolt by Lambert Simnel who pretended to be the Earl of Warwick and claimed the throne. He was crowned king in Dublin, then invaded England. Henry defeated him at Stoke, and put him to work in the royal kitchens as punishment.

FIRM GOVERNMENT

To begin with, Henry's hold on power was weak, and he fought several wars to defend his crown from France and Scotland. But he strengthened his position by a treaty with France, and by reducing the power of the nobles. Helped by his chancellor, John Morton, Henry also ruthlessly rebuilt the royal finances, introducing new taxes on savings and leaving a huge fortune to his son, Henry.

> He was of a high mind, and loved his own will and his own way; as one that revered himself, and would reign indeed.

FRANCIS BACON, HISTORY OF THE REIGN OF HENRY VII

1486	Marries Elizabeth of York	**1503**	Death of Prince Arthur	**1509**	Death of Henry VII
1487	Revolt by Lambert Simnel	**1503**	Death of Elizabeth of York		

1509-1547
HENRY VIII

Henry became heir to the throne on the death of his brother, Arthur. When his father died in 1509, he became king. He married Catherine of Aragon, his brother's widow and daughter of the Spanish king and queen. Henry VIII remains one of history's most colourful kings, famous for his many wives and his reformation of the English Church.

EARLY REIGN

As a young man, Henry was handsome and athletic. Though well-educated, he preferred hunting and jousting to ruling, and left the government mainly in the hands of his chancellor, Cardinal Thomas Wolsey. Wolsey governed well but fell out of favour when he failed to get the king a divorce from his first wife, Catherine of Aragon. He died in 1530, before he could be tried for treason.

TURNING POINT

LOOTING THE MONASTERIES

To show his authority, Henry raided hundreds of monasteries throughout England and stripped them of riches and land. This made him extremely wealthy but meant that many priceless treasures were lost or destroyed.

TIMELINE

1491 Birth of Henry VIII

1509 (April) Becomes King of England; Marries Catherine of Aragon

1513 Battle of Flodden Field

1533 Birth of future Elizabeth I

DID YOU KNOW?

In later life, Henry's health began to fail. He injured his leg while jousting and this made exercise difficult. He became so fat that he could not move without being helped.

Divorced,
beheaded,
died.
Divorced,
beheaded,
survived.

BREAK WITH ROME

Henry and Catherine had a daughter, Mary (later Mary I), but Henry was desperate for a son and heir. He decided to divorce Catherine and marry Anne Boleyn. As a Catholic, he had to ask permission from the head of the Catholic Church – the Pope in Rome. The Pope refused. Henry broke with Rome and declared himself head of the Church of England. He divorced Catherine and married Anne. She later gave birth to a daughter who was to become Elizabeth I. Henry went on to marry a further four times, having a son, Edward (later Edward VI), with his third wife, Jane Seymour.

TURNING POINT

SIX WIVES

1. **Catherine of Aragon**
   (married 1509; divorced 1533)
2. **Anne Boleyn**
   (married 1533; beheaded 1536)
3. **Jane Seymour**
   (married 1536; died 1537)
4. **Anne of Cleves**
   (married January 1540; divorced July 1540)
5. **Catherine Howard**
   (married 1540; beheaded 1541)
6. **Catherine Parr**
   (married 1543)

> His fingers were one mass of jewelled rings, and around his neck he wore a gold collar from which hung a diamond as big as a walnut. His clothes were magnificent to match-precious metals sprinkled everywhere.

CONTEMPORARY ACCOUNT OF HENRY VIII

1534 Act of Supremacy	**1537** Birth of Prince Edward	**1546** Makes peace with France
1536 Act of Union between Wales and England	**1544** Act of Succession	**1547** Death of Henry VIII in London

1547-1553
EDWARD VI

When a sick and bloated Henry VIII died in 1547, his only son, Edward, became king. He was just nine years old. The country was ruled on his behalf first by his uncle, the Duke of Somerset, then by the Duke of Northumberland. But, in 1552, Edward caught tuberculosis, and died the following year.

LADY JANE GREY

On Edward's death, the rightful heir to the throne was his sister, Mary. But she was a Catholic, and the Duke of Northumberland was determined to stop her from ruling. He quickly proclaimed his 15-year-old daughter-in-law, Lady Jane Grey, a Protestant, queen. Her reign was the shortest in English history. Nine days later, Mary marched on London to claim the throne, and later had Jane executed.

TURNING POINT

PROTESTANT REFORM

Under Henry's changes, England became a Protestant country. In 1549, the Catholic mass was banned, and the First Book of Common Prayer introduced. English replaced Latin as the language of church services.

TIMELINE

1537 Birth of Edward VI; birth of Jane Grey

1553 Death of Edward VI; Lady Jane Grey becomes Queen (July)

1553 Mary I becomes Queen (July)

1554 Lady Jane Grey beheaded

He was a likely lad of quick, ready and
well-developed mind, remarkably so for his age.

1553-1558
MARY I

Mary was born in 1516, the only surviving child of Henry VIII and Catherine of Aragon. When Henry married Anne Boleyn, Mary was stripped of her title of princess and forced to become lady-in-waiting to her younger, half-sister, Elizabeth. She was later reconciled with her father, and named heir after her brother, Edward.

PROTESTANT PERSECUTION

Mary was a devout Catholic. She was determined to bring back Catholicism as the official religion of England. She freed many Catholic priests who had been imprisoned, and persecuted Protestants, having hundreds burned alive at the stake. In 1554, Mary married the Catholic Philip of Spain (later King Philip II of Spain), whom many of her subjects mistrusted. They believed, rightly, that he would try to seize control of England (see pages 77). Mary died in 1558, with no heir to carry on her work.

TURNING POINT

LOSS OF CALAIS

Mary's reign was also marked by an unsuccessful war with France. This led to the loss of Calais, England's last possession on France, in January 1558.

TIMELINE

1516 Birth of Mary I	**1553** Becomes Queen of England	**1558** Calais captured by the French
	1554 Marries Philip of Spain	**1558** Death of Mary (November)

DID YOU KNOW?
Mary I was nicknamed
'Bloody Mary'
because of her
persecution
of the
Protestants.

1558-1603
ELIZABETH I

The daughter of Henry VIII and Anne Boleyn, Elizabeth came to the throne in 1558, and ruled England for the next 45 years. Clever, shrewd and ruthless, Elizabeth established herself as one of England's greatest monarchs, transforming it from a poor and divided country into a prosperous trading nation.

RELIGIOUS SETTLEMENT

When Elizabeth came to the throne, England was divided by religion. Under Henry VIII, it had become a Protestant country, while most of Europe remained Catholic. Under Mary I (see page 72), England briefly became Catholic again, and Protestants were persecuted. Elizabeth tried to end the confusion. Between 1559–1563, she passed the laws of Religious Settlement and returned England to the Protestant faith. The Church of England, of which she became Supreme Governor, remains today.

TURNING POINT

POOR LAWS

Many people in Elizabethan England were very poor. To help them, Elizabeth's government passed a series of Poor Laws. People who were better-off had to pay a tax to support the needy, and towns had to provide work for the unemployed.

TIMELINE

1533	Birth of Elizabeth 1 in London	**1536**	Execution of Anne Boleyn	**1553**	Mary I becomes queen
		1547	Edward VI becomes king	**1558**	Becomes Queen of England

DID YOU KNOW?

There are many portraits of Elizabeth I, though she did not pose for any of them. Even so, if she disliked a particular picture, she had it destroyed.

Ye GLOBE

Hamlet, Prince of Denmark

WILLIAM SHAKESPEARE

DID YOU KNOW?

Elizabeth never married, though she had many suitors. It is thought that she wanted to marry Robert Dudley, Earl of Leicester but was put off by her advisors when Dudley's wife died mysteriously in a fall down stairs.

> I do not so much rejoice that God hath made me to be a Queen, as to be a Queen over so thankful a people.

FROM THE GOLDEN SPEECH, 1601

THE SPANISH ARMADA

Later in her reign, Elizabeth faced another threat. England and Spain, a powerful, Catholic country were bitter enemies. King Philip II of Spain, Mary's husband, was furious when Elizabeth sent an army to help the Dutch in their fight against the Spanish. In 1588, he sent a massive fleet of ships – the Armada – to destroy the English Navy and put a Catholic ruler on the throne. But gale-force winds drove the Armada ships off course and the danger of invasion passed.

TURNING POINT

A GOLDEN AGE

Elizabeth's reign became known as a golden age in English history. Theatres flourished, with writers, including William Shakespeare, putting on plays for the queen. It was also an exciting time in exploration, with adventurers, such as Francis Drake, making daring voyages.

1559 –63 Passes the laws of Religious Settlement	**1564** Birth of William Shakespeare	**1588** Spanish Armada defeated
1563 –1601 Poor Laws passed	**1587** Execution of Mary, Queen of Scots	**1603** Death of Elizabeth in London

1603-1625
JAMES I

Elizabeth I died in 1603 without any children, and James VI of Scotland became King James I of England. He was the first Stuart King of England. Born in Edinburgh in 1566, James was the son of Mary, Queen of Scots. When he was a year old, his mother was forced to abdicate in his favour and regents ruled for him.

DIVINE RIGHT OF KINGS

James I soon proved unpopular with his English subjects. He strongly believed in the 'divine right of kings', whereby kings only answer to God. As a result, he refused to share his power with Parliament, undermining the strong government put in place by Elizabeth I. He also angered people by raising taxes, and by trying to marry his son, Charles, to the daughter of the Catholic king of Spain.

TURNING POINT

KING JAMES' BIBLE

One of James' lasting legacies was a new translation of the Bible (from the Greek) that was easier for people to read and understand. Completed in 1611, it remained the standard English version of the Bible for more than 250 years.

TIMELINE

1566 Birth of James

1567 Murder of James' father, Lord Darnley

1567 Becomes King James VI of Scotland

DID YOU KNOW?
James I was known as 'the wisest fool in Christendom' because he appeared foolish, although he was well educated.

GUY FAWKES

DID YOU KNOW?

There were many plots against James and he lived in constant fear of being assassinated, wearing padded clothes to protect himself from being stabbed.

His beard was very thin, his tongue too large for his mouth, which ever made him speak full in the mouth, and made him drink very uncomely...

CONTEMPORARY ACCOUNT BY SIR ANTHONY WELDON

GUNPOWDER PLOT

In November 1605, a group of Catholics hatched a plot to blow up the king when he opened Parliament. They wanted a Catholic monarch on the throne. They dug a tunnel under the House of Lords and filled a cellar with gunpowder. But the plot was foiled when one of the group, Guy Fawkes, was discovered by the guards. Fawkes was tortured and hanged, along with his co-conspirators, though their daring plot is still remembered.

TURNING POINT

PILGRIM FATHERS

In 1620, a group of about 100 Puritans (Protestants) sailed from England in a ship, called the *Mayflower*. Unhappy with the religious laws at home, they were bound for a new life in America. Known as the Pilgrim Fathers, they founded one of the English colonies that later became the first states of the USA.

1589	Marries Anne of Denmark	1605	Gunpowder plot	1611	King James's Bible
1603	Becomes King James I of England	1606	Gunpowder plotters executed	1620	The Mayflower sails to America
				1625	Death of James I

1625-1649
CHARLES I

The second son of James I, Charles only became king because his older brother, Henry, died. Like his father, Charles believed that it was his divine right to rule (see page 78), and resented the way that Parliament tried to limit his power. This was to lead to a Civil War which tore England apart.

CLASHES WITH PARLIAMENT

In 1629, Charles dismissed Parliament and, for the next 11 years, ran the country by himself. Without Parliament's backing, he struggled to raise money and resorted to unpopular methods, such as 'Ship Money', a tax raised on coastal counties. Charles extended this to all counties, near the sea, or not. Charles was finally forced to recall Parliament in 1640 to ask for money to fight a Scottish rebellion. Unsurprisingly, Parliament was in no mood to agree to his demands.

TURNING POINT

ENGLISH CIVIL WAR

In 1642, Civil War broke out between the Royalists and the Parliamentarians. The Royalists won the first battle of the war, at Edgehill. But their luck was to change. At the Battle of Naseby in 1645, MP Oliver Cromwell's 'New Model Army' crushed the Royalists. Charles was captured and imprisoned. He was executed January 1649.

TIMELINE

	1625 Becomes King of England & Scotland	**1642** Civil War breaks out
1600 Birth of Charles I	**1628** Petition of Rights	**1645** Battle of Naseby

DID YOU KNOW?
On the day of his execution, Charles wore two shirts in case he shivered in the cold. He did not want the people to think that he was trembling with fear.

OLIVER CROMWELL

DID YOU KNOW?

The Royalists were also known as 'Cavaliers' because they wore their hair long, like the king. The Parliamentarians were also called 'Roundheads' because they cut their hair short and wore round helmets.

> I tell you, we will cut off his head with the crown upon it.

CROMWELL AT THE TRIAL OF CHARLES I

INTERREGNUM

After Charles I's death in 1649, the monarchy was abolished and England declared a republic. This period, called the Interregnum ('between reigns') lasted until 1660. The Parliamentarian leader, Oliver Cromwell, became Lord Protector in 1653. He ruthlessly put down rebellions and imposed his own strict, religious values on the country. Inns and theatres were closed down; gambling, betting, and even Christmas celebrations were banned. Cromwell died in 1658.

TURNING POINT

OLIVER CROMWELL

Cromwell was born in 1599 into a fairly well-to-do family. He studied at Cambridge University, then became an MP. A deeply religious Puritan, Cromwell believed that his actions were guided by God. When Civil War broke out, he showed himself to be a superb soldier and military leader, masterminding the defeat of the king.

1649 Execution of Charles I	**1653** Cromwell becomes Lord Protector	**1660** Interregnum period ends
1649 Start of Interregnum period	**1658** Death of Cromwell	**1660** Restoration of monarch

1660–1685
CHARLES II

Charles was born in 1630, the oldest surviving son of Charles I. As a teenager, he fought in the Civil War but was forced to flee into exile in Europe. After his father's execution, he tried to win back the throne but was defeated by Cromwell at the Battle of Worcester. Again, he was forced to escape into exile, in disguise.

RESTORATION OF THE MONARCHY

Oliver Cromwell died in 1658, and two years later, Charles was invited back to England to become king. Nicknamed the 'Merry Monarch', he proved to be a popular king. He was fun-loving and tolerant, overturning many of Cromwell's strict laws. He was also interested in art, poetry, the theatre and science. His reign saw England become rich and powerful because of trade and its new colonies abroad.

TURNING POINT

TREATY OF DOVER

In 1670, Charles signed a secret treaty with Louis XIV of France. In return for financial help, Charles agreed to support France's war against the Dutch, and to convert to Catholicism. He eventually became a Catholic on his deathbed.

TIMELINE

1630 Birth of Charles II

1651 Battle of Worcester

1660 Restoration of monarch

1660 Becomes King of England and Scotland 👉

DID YOU KNOW?
Legend says that, after
the Battle of Worcester,
Charles was forced
to spend the day
hiding in an
oak tree.

NELL GWYN

DID YOU KNOW?

Famous for his good looks, Charles II was married to a Portuguese princess, Catherine of Braganza, but he also had 14 known mistresses. His favourite was a former actress and orange-seller, called Nell Gwyn.

"We have a pretty witty king, whose word no man relies on; He never said a foolish thing, Nor ever did a wise one."

JOHN WILMOT, EARL OF ROCHESTER

LONDON IN FLAMES

Disaster struck London early in Charles's reign. In 1665, the city was hit by bubonic plague, spread to humans by fleas living on infected rats. In an attempt to stop the plague from spreading, victims were locked in their houses and crosses drawn on their doors. Despite this, around a fifth of Londoners died. A year later, the city was devastated by a huge fire. It raged for four days, destroying more than 13,000 buildings.

TURNING POINT

THE POPISH PLOT

Despite Charles' own beliefs, discrimination against Catholics continued. In 1678, Protestant clergyman, Titus Oates, gave details of a Catholic plot to murder the king and put his openly Catholic brother, James, on the throne. In the following hysteria, 35 Catholics were executed. In fact, the so-called 'Popish Plot' never existed.

1665	**Plague strikes London**
1666	**The Great Fire of London**

1670	**Treaty of Dover**
1678	**The Popish Plot**

1685	**Death of Charles II**

1685–1688
JAMES II

James II came to the throne in 1685, on the death of his brother, Charles II. A devout Catholic, James set about trying to overturn anti-Catholic laws and restore England as a Catholic country. This led to conflict with the Protestant Church of England, and with Parliament.

GLORIOUS REVOLUTION

The Protestants hoped that, when James died, the throne would pass to Mary, his Protestant daughter. But, in 1688, James's second wife gave birth to a son who would be brought up as a Catholic. A group of leading Protestants invited Mary and her Dutch husband, William of Orange, to England to overthrow James. This event became known as the Glorious Revolution. Facing defeat, James fled to France. In 1689, William and Mary were crowned King and Queen. A year later, James returned with an army but was defeated at the Battle of the Boyne in Ireland (see page 92).

TURNING POINT

DECLARATION OF INDULGENCE

In 1688, James made himself more unpopular with Protestants by issuing a Declaration of Indulgence, aimed at allowing Catholics freedom to worship. He instructed the Protestant clergy to read it from their pulpits. If they did not, they were prosecuted.

TIMELINE

1633	Birth of James II	1673	Marries Mary of Modena	1688	Deposed
1660	Marries Anne Hyde	1685	Becomes King of England and Scotland	1689	William and Mary crowned king and que
				1690	Battle of the Boyne
				1701	Death of James II

DID YOU KNOW?

The city of New York in the USA was named in James's honour. Before he became king, he was the Duke of York.

1689–1702
WILLIAM & MARY

In 1689, Dutch prince, William of Orange and his wife, Mary, were invited to England to overthrow James II (see page 90). They were crowned king (William III) and queen (Mary II) soon afterwards. Later that year, James II returned from exile with an army but was defeated by William at the Battle of the Boyne in Ireland, in 1690.

A ROYAL MARRIAGE

William was born in the Hague, Holland, in 1650, the son of William II of Orange and Mary Stuart, daughter of Charles I (see page 82). His father died a few days before his birth. In 1677, he married Mary, his cousin and daughter of James II. Mary died of smallpox in 1694, at the age of 32 years old, leaving William grief-stricken. The couple had no children and, when William died in 1702, the throne passed to Mary's sister, Anne (see page 96).

TURNING POINT

BATTLE OF THE BOYNE

The Battle of the Boyne took place on 1 July 1690 on the east coast of Ireland, between the Protestant William III and the Catholic James II. James was supported by the Irish Catholics who resented Protestant settlers taking their land. James was defeated and fled back to France. The battle is still celebrated by Irish Protestants today.

TIMELINE

1662	**Birth of Mary**
1677	**Marriage of William and Mary**
1650	**Birth of William**
1688	**William lands in England**

DID YOU KNOW?
Mary was very fond of gardening and planned the gardens at Hampton Court Palace with Sir Christopher Wren.

MARY

DID YOU KNOW?
William died in a riding accident, when his horse stumbled over a molehill.

> The liberties of England and the Protestant religion I will maintain.

WILLIAM III

JOINT REIGN

William and Mary became joint rulers of England, Scotland and Ireland under terms set out by Parliament in a 'Declaration of Rights' (later 'Bill of Rights'). This limited the power of the monarchy and barred Catholics, or those married to Catholics, from succeeding. During the reign, William's main concern was fighting the French. He wanted to stop King Louis XIV from taking control of Europe. Fighting continued through the 1690s but, by 1697, both sides were exhausted and a temporary truce was called.

TURNING POINT

MASSACRE OF GLENCOE

Some of the Scottish clans continued to support James II. Their chiefs were ordered to swear an oath of allegiance to William and Mary. The chief of the McDonalds of Glencoe missed the deadline, and 40 of his clan were massacred by soldiers, pretending to be their guests.

1689 Become king and queen	**1692** Massacre of Glencoe	**1701** War of the Spanish Succession
1690 Battle of the Boyne	**1694** Death of Mary	**1702** Death of William

1702–1714
ANNE

The last of the Stuart monarchs, Anne was born in 1665. She was the daughter of James II, and sister of Mary II. She had been raised as a Protestant and, on the death of her brother-in-law, William III, became queen. Despite having 19 children, Anne died without an heir, and the throne passed to George of Hanover (see pages 98–99).

SPANISH SUCCESSION

Shortly after Anne came to the throne, England and France clashed in the War of the Spanish Succession. England wanted to stop the French king's candidate becoming King of Spain. Under the Duke of Marlborough's brilliant leadership, England won a string of spectacular victories and became a leading power in Europe. In 1713, the Treaty of Utrecht ended the war.

TURNING POINT

ACT OF UNION

In 1707, the Act of Union formally united the kingdoms of England and Scotland and the Scottish government transferred to London. Anne became the first ruler of Great Britain.

TIMELINE

1665	Birth of Anne
1683	Marries George of Denmark
1702	Becomes queen
1713	Treaty of Utrecht
1714	Death of Anne in London

1714-1727
GEORGE I

Under the 1701 Act of Succession, George of Hanover (Germany) became king on Anne's death. A great-grandson of James I, he was her closest suitable Protestant relative. George arrived in London in 1714, speaking no English and knowing little about his new kingdom. The following year, he faced a rebellion by the Jacobites, supporters of James Stuart.

SOUTH SEA BUBBLE

In 1720, the South Sea Company collapsed and thousands of investors were ruined. The scandal was known as the South Sea Bubble. George had been heavily involved, and his popularity fell even further. Robert Walpole, the First Lord of the Treasury, took advantage to become Britain's powerful first Prime Minister.

TURNING POINT

JAMES STUART

James Stuart (1688–1766) was the Catholic son of James II and his second wife, Mary Modena. He was also known as the 'Old Pretender'. His son, Charles, or 'Bonnie Prince Charlie', was the 'Young Pretender'. Their supporters, known as the Jacobites, believed that they were the rightful heirs to the throne.

TIMELINE

1660 Birth of George I in Germany	**1682** Marries Sophia **1714** Becomes King of Great Britain & Ireland	**1715** Jacobite rising **1727** Death of George I in Germany

DID YOU KNOW?

When George I arrived in London in 1714, he brought 18 cooks with him but only one servant to wash his clothes.

1727–1760
GEORGE II

George II was born in Germany in 1683. When he was four, his father imprisoned his mother, and she never saw her children again. George never forgave his father, and avoided being in his company. He became king in 1727. By the time of his death in 1760, Britain was on its way to becoming a major world power, with expanding colonies in North America and India.

PEACE AND WAR

The first 12 years of George II's reign were peaceful but, from 1739, Britain was almost constantly at war in Europe. A fine soldier, George himself led his troops against the French at the Battle of Dettingen in 1743, the last British monarch to do so. In Scotland, the Jacobites, led by James Stuart's son, Charles ('Bonnie Prince Charlie'), rebelled again in 1745. The following year, they were heavily defeated by George's son, Frederick, at the Battle of Culloden.

TURNING POINT

WAR OF JENKINS' EAR

In 1739, Britain declared war on Spain and fighting continued for the next nine years. The war was partly triggered by Robert Jenkins, captain of a British merchant ship. He claimed his ear had been cut off by the Spanish in a skirmish at sea.

TIMELINE

1683	Birth of George II
1705	Marries Caroline of Ansbach
1727	Becomes king
1737	Death of Queen Caroline
1746	Battle of Culloden
1756	Start of Seven Years' War
1760	Death of George II

DID YOU KNOW?

George II fell out with his eldest son, Frederick, and banished him from court. Frederick died in 1751 after being hit by a cricket ball.

1760–1820
GEORGE III

George III was the son of Frederick, Prince of Wales, and became king in 1760 when his grandfather, George II, died. He was the first Hanoverian monarch to be born and raised in England, and the first to use English as his first language. His 60-year reign was a time of great change, with Britain losing its colonies in America but gaining a huge empire.

WAR IN AMERICA

In 1773, a group of American colonists staged an extraordinary protest against the high taxes imposed on them by the British government. They dumped 342 chests of tea into Boston harbour. Two years after the so-called 'Boston Tea Party', the American War of Independence began, with the colonists fighting the British. The British were finally defeated in 1781, and forced to recognise American independence.

TURNING POINT

AGE OF ENLIGHTENMENT

George III was a great supporter of the sciences and arts, helping to found the Royal Academy. He helped to bring the Enlightenment – a movement that believed in the power of learning – to Britain from Europe.

TIMELINE

1738 Birth of George III in London	**1761** Marries Charlotte of Mecklenburg-Strelitz	**1773** Boston Tea Party
1760 Becomes king		**1788** George falls ill

DID YOU KNOW?
It was during George III's reign that Captain James Cook set off on the first of his historic voyages to the Pacific in 1769.

ADMIRAL LORD NELSON

DID YOU KNOW?

In 1812, Prime Minister, Spencer Perceval, was shot dead in the House of Commons by a man with a grudge against the government. He is the only British Prime Minister to have been assassinated.

> I was the last person to consent to the separation (of Britain and America), but I will be the first to accept the friendship of the United States as an independent power.

GEORGE III

MAD KING GEORGE?

In 1788, George fell seriously ill. It was thought that he had gone mad but he may have been suffering from an inherited illness, called porphyria. He recovered but, in 1810, suffered a total collapse. His eldest son, George, Prince of Wales, was appointed regent. Blind, deaf, and talking constantly to himself, George III was kept locked up by himself in Windsor Castle until his death in 1820.

TURNING POINT

BATTLE OF TRAFALGAR

In 1805, Admiral Lord Nelson led the British to victory against the French and Spanish in the Battle of Trafalgar. It was Britain's most important naval victory of the Napoleonic Wars. Nelson was killed in the battle but remains one of Britain's greatest war heroes.

1789	French Revolution
1801	Union of Great Britain and Ireland
1805	Battle of Trafalgar
1820	Death of George III in London

1820–1830
GEORGE IV

Born in 1762, George was the eldest son of George III. Handsome and intelligent, he was a leading figure in fashionable society and a great supporter of the arts. He loved drinking and gambling, and his lifestyle brought him into conflict with his father. However, in 1811, when George III was taken ill, George became Prince Regent and ruled on his behalf.

KING GEORGE

George formally became king in 1820 when George III died. Shortly afterwards, he put his wife, Caroline, on trial. Their marriage had been a disaster and he now tried to divorce her for being unfaithful. He failed but had her banned from his coronation the following year. George did not take much interest in politics but was forced to agree to the Catholic Relief Act in 1829. This allowed Catholics to become MPs. In George's later life, he became hugely overweight and his health suffered.

TURNING POINT

BOBBIES ON THE BEAT

During George's reign, the first police force began walking the beat in London. The force was created by Prime Minister, Robert Peel, and officers became known as 'bobbies'. Unpopular at first, they were very successful in cutting crime in London.

TIMELINE

1795	Marries Caroline of Brunswick
1762	Birth of George IV
1815	Battle of Waterloo
1820	Becomes king
1829	Catholic Relief Act
1830	Death of George IV in Windsor

DID YOU KNOW?

The Regency is the period of history between 1811–1820. It gets it name because these were the years when George acted as Prince Regent.

1830–1837
WILLIAM IV

The third son of George III, William never expected to be king. But George IV's only daughter died in 1817, followed by William's older brother, Frederick. This left William to succeed in 1830. Nicknamed the 'Sailor King', he had joined the Navy at the age of 13 and risen to the rank of admiral. His reign saw the ending of slavery in the British Empire.

REFORM CRISIS

In 1830, the Tories lost the general election and the Whigs came to power. The Whigs wanted to reform parliament, to make the election of MPs fairer. They tried to pass a law, allowing more people to vote, but it was bitterly opposed by the House of Lords and the Tories. William opposed the bill but, wisely, did not stand in its way. The Great Reform Act became law in 1832, extending the vote to a further 250,000 people.

TURNING POINT

TOLPUDDLE MARTYRS

In 1834, six farm workers from Dorset in England formed a trade union to protest against the low wages they were being paid. They were arrested, put on trial and sentenced to be transported to Australia. They became known as the Tolpuddle Martyrs.

TIMELINE

1765	Birth of William IV	1830	Becomes king	1833	Abolition of slavery in British Empire
1789	Becomes Duke of Clarence	1832	Great Reform Act	1834	Poor Law Act
				1837	Death of William

DID YOU KNOW?
William IV earned the embarrassing nickname 'Silly Billy' because of his habit of making long and rambling speeches.

1837-1901
VICTORIA

Victoria was born in 1819, the only child of Edward, Duke of Kent. After an unhappy childhood, she succeeded her uncle, William IV, to the throne in 1837, at the age of 18. Her reign lasted for the next 64 years, the longest of any British monarch. During it, Britain was transformed, with trade and industry thriving, and great changes in education, science and society.

BRITISH EMPIRE

Victoria ruled over the largest empire ever known, said to cover a quarter of the globe. It included Canada, Australia, New Zealand, India and large parts of Africa. In 1857, after the Indian Mutiny against British rule, the government of India passed to the British Crown. Victoria was given the title 'Empress of India, although she never visited the country. The late 19th century also saw the 'Scramble for Africa', a struggle between various European nations for territory in Africa.

TURNING POINT

POTATO FAMINE

In 1845–1851, Ireland's potato crop was devastated by disease. In the famine that followed, millions of people starved to death. Poor Irish tenants who could not pay their rents turned against their wealthy English landlords, and a campaign began for Irish self-rule.

TIMELINE

| 1819 | Birth of Victoria | 1840 | Marries Prince Albert | 1853 | Start of Crimean War |
| 1837 | Becomes queen | 1851 | Great Exhibition | 1857 | Indian Mutiny |

The important thing is
not what they think
of me, but what I
think of them.

VICTORIA

DID YOU KNOW?
Prince Albert introduced
the customs of sending
Christmas cards
and decorating
Christmas trees
to Britain from
Germany.

PRINCE ALBERT

PRINCE ALBERT

In 1840, Victoria married her German first cousin, Prince Albert. The couple were devoted to each other, and had nine children. Intelligent and hard-working, Albert oversaw the Great Exhibition of 1851 to show off British inventions and technology, and was eventually given the title of Prince Consort. But tragedy struck in 1861, when Albert caught typhoid and died, aged just 42. Victoria was devastated. She refused to appear in public, and wore black for the rest of her life. Gradually, she was persuaded to come out of mourning, and her Golden Jubilee (1887) and Diamond Jubilee (1897) were huge celebrations.

DID YOU KNOW?

In 1870, the Education Act made it compulsory and free for children under 12 to go to school. Before this, poor children often worked sweeping chimneys or in factories.

TURNING POINT

CRIMEAN WAR

In 1854, Britain went to war with Russia to stop it expanding its territory in the Crimea (modern-day Ukraine). Thousands of soldiers died in battle, or later from infections caught in the filthy hospitals. A woman, called Florence Nightingale, cleaned up the hospitals and helped to cut the number of deaths.

1861 Death of Prince Albert	**1887** Golden Jubilee	**1897** Diamond Jubilee
1870 Education Act	**1893** Founding of Independent Labour Party	**1901** Death of Victoria

1901–1910
EDWARD VII

The eldest son of Albert and Victoria, Edward VII had a strict upbringing to prepare him for becoming king one day. By the time he came to the throne in 1901, he was already nearly 60 years old. Good natured and stylish, he loved good food, good wine and horseracing. In contrast to Victoria's reign, his was full of colour and ceremony, and he was a hugely popular king.

ENTENTE CORDIALE

Edward's charming manner made him a natural diplomat and he made several foreign visits. Acting as ambassador for Britain was a new role for a monarch, and is still very important today. In 1904, he helped to bring about the Entente Cordiale – an agreement between Britain and its long-time enemy, France, settling the two countries' disputes about territory.

TURNING POINT

VOTES FOR WOMEN

In Edwardian Britain, women were still not treated as equal to men. In 1903, Emmeline Pankhurst and her group of Suffragettes began campaigning for women to be allowed to vote. This finally happened in 1928.

TIMELINE

1841	Birth of Edward VII
1863	Marries Alexandra of Denmark
1901	Becomes king
1904	Entente Cordiale
1910	Death of Edward VII in Buckingham Palace

DID YOU KNOW?
Christened Albert Edward, and called 'Bertie' by his family and friends, the new king announced that he would be known as Edward VII.

1910–1936
GEORGE V

George V came to the throne in 1910, on the death of his father, Edward VII. A second son, he had been planning a career in the Royal Navy, when his elder brother died suddenly. In 1893, George married his late brother's fiancée, Princess Mary of Teck. They had a long and happy marriage, and six children. George was a steady and popular king.

WORLD WAR I

In 1914, Britain was plunged into World War I against Germany, led by Kaiser Wilhelm I, George's cousin. The King and Queen gained respect for their many visits to the troops, and to military hospitals and factories. Four years later, the Germans were forced to surrender. More than 20 million people died in the war. In the Battle of the Somme alone (1916), 420,000 British soldiers lost their lives.

TURNING POINT

HOUSE OF WINDSOR

In 1917 George V changed his surname from the German, Saxe-Coburg-Gotha, to Windsor because of the strong anti-German feeling in Britain during World War I.

TIMELINE

1865	Birth of George V	**1910** Becomes king	**1924** First Labour government
1893	Marries Mary of Teck	**1914** World War I breaks out	**1931** Great Depression
		1918 End of World War I	**1936** Death of George V

DID YOU KNOW?
George V's main hobby was stamp collecting, and he built up a large and valuable collection.

1936
EDWARD VIII

Edward VIII came to the throne in January 1936 when his father, George V, died. Shortly after Edward announced that he wanted to marry Wallis Simpson, an American who had been divorced twice. The Prime Minister told him that she could not become Queen and so, in December 1936, Edward abdicated. He had been king for less than a year.

DUKE OF WINDSOR

Edward married Wallis Simpson the following year, and the couple were given the titles, Duke and Duchess of Windsor. During World War II, Edward was appointed governor of the Bahamas but the couple spent the rest of their lives in France. His family never forgave him and he only paid short visits to England. He died in 1972, and was buried in Windsor.

TURNING POINT

ABDICATION

Edward VIII announced his abdication in a radio broadcast on 11 December 1936. In his speech, he said: 'You must believe me when I tell you that I have found it impossible to carry the heavy burden of responsibility and to discharge my duties as king as I would wish to do without the help and support of the woman I love.'

TIMELINE

1894	Birth of Edward VIII	1936	Abdicates (December)
1936	Becomes king	1937	Marries Wallis Simpson
		1972	Death of Edward in France
		1986	Death of the Duchess of Windsor

DID YOU KNOW?
Edward VIII's full name was Edward Albert Christian George Andrew Patrick David, though he was known to his family as David.

1936-1952
GEORGE VI

The second son of George V, George served in the Navy and Air Force, and became Duke of York in 1920. He married Lady Elizabeth Bowes-Lyon in 1923. When his brother, Edward VIII, abdicated in 1936, George VI became king unexpectedly. A shy man, he proved a strong and popular king during wartime, and helped to repair the royal family's damaged reputation.

COMMONWEALTH OF NATIONS

From the 1930s, the British Empire began to break up. Many former colonies, such as Australia, Canada and India, became independent. These countries joined the Commonwealth of Nations, an organisation set up to promote world peace and trade. George VI was recognised as its first head.

TURNING POINT

INDIAN INDEPENDENCE

In 1947, India finally gained independence from Britain, after a struggle lasting many years. It was led by Mahatma Gandhi, who became a national hero. But freedom was bittersweet. The country was divided into two – India and Pakistan – along religious lines. Millions of people were uprooted or died in the fighting that broke out.

TIMELINE

1895 Birth of George VI	**1923** Marries Lady Elizabeth Bowes-Lyon

1936 Becomes king	
1939 World War II breaks out	

DID YOU KNOW?
George VI was a keen tennis player and competed in the Wimbledon Championships in 1926.

WINSTON CHURCHILL

DID YOU KNOW?

The George Cross is a medal awarded to civilians for great acts of bravery. It was created by George VI in 1940 to reward people's courage during the Blitz.

'You can be assured that I will do my best to clear up the inevitable mess, if the whole fabric does not crumble under the shock and strain of it all.'

GEORGE VI ON BECOMING KING

WORLD WAR II

On 3 September 1939, Britain declared war on Germany and World War II began. George VI became an important figurehead, visiting the troops to help boost their spirits. In September 1940, the 'Blitz' began. For the next nine months, London was bombed nightly by German planes. Despite the danger, George VI and his family refused to leave London, even when Buckingham Palace was hit.

TURNING POINT

WINSTON CHURCHILL

Winston Churchill became Prime Minister in 1940 and led Britain through the war. Using rousing speeches, he united the country and made the British people feel that they could fight, and beat, the Nazis.

1940 Winston Churchill becomes Prime Minister

1940 Battle of Britain

1945 End of World War II

1952 Death of George VI

1952-
ELIZABETH II

Elizabeth II became queen of the United Kingdom of Great Britain and Northern Ireland in 1952. Born in 1926, she became heir to the throne when her father, George VI, became king unexpectedly in 1936. She heard about her father's death in 1952 while she was on safari in Kenya. Her coronation the following year was the first to be shown on television.

FAMILY LIFE

Elizabeth, known as 'Lilibet', and her younger sister, Margaret, had a happy childhood. But, when war broke out in 1939, they were evacuated to Windsor Castle. Elizabeth wanted to help in the war effort, and trained as a driver in the Women's Auxiliary Territorial Service. In November 1947, she married Philip Mountbatten who became Duke of Edinburgh. They have four children – Charles, Anne, Andrew and Edward.

TURNING POINT

ANNUS HORRIBILIS

In a speech, the Queen described 1992 as her 'annus horribilis' or 'horrible year'. This was the year when Windsor Castle was badly damaged by fire, Princess Anne got divorced, and Prince Charles and Princess Diana separated.

TIMELINE

1926	Birth of Elizabeth II	**1947**	Marries Philip Mountbatten
		1948	Birth of Prince Charles
1952	Becomes queen		
1977	Silver Jubilee		

DID YOU KNOW?
The Queen is very fond of dogs, especially Pembroke Welsh corgis. She has owned more than 30 corgis.

DID YOU KNOW?
Prince Charles (born 1948) is Elizabeth II's eldest son and heir. He became Prince of Wales in 1969. When Charles becomes king, his eldest son, William (born 1982), will become Prince of Wales.

• CHARLES & WILLIAM •

LATER REIGN

For almost 60 years, Elizabeth II has taken her duties very seriously, both at home and abroad. Although her role is largely formal, and she has no real political power, she is greatly respected and loved. Her long reign has seen enormous changes in Britain, including the monarchy being in the media spotlight. She has also had to face scandals in her own family, with three of her children getting divorced. She celebrated her Golden Jubilee in 2002, and in 2016, could become Britain's longest-reigning monarch.

TURNING POINT

QUEEN MOTHER

Elizabeth II's mother, Queen Elizabeth, the Queen Mother, died peacefully in her sleep in March 2002. She was 101 years old. A hugely popular member of the royal family, she carried out her royal duties until just a few months before her death.

' I declare before you all that my whole life whether it be long or short shall be devoted to your service... '

QUEEN ELIZABETH II

1981	Wedding of Charles and Diana	1992	Annus horribilis	2002	Golden Jubilee
1982	Birth of Prince William	1997	Death of Princess Diana	2002	Death of Queen Mother
				2006	80th birthday

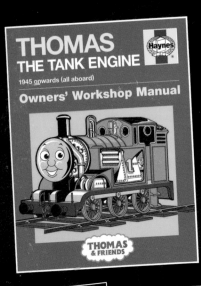